Journey into PRAYER

Milton L. Rudnick

CONCORDIA PUBLISHING HOUSE · SAINT LOUIS

TO DAUGHTER DEB,

WHO IS AN ANSWER TO PRAYER

AND WHO HAS A HEART FOR PRAYER

3558 S. Jefferson Ave., St. Louis, MO 63118-3968

1-800-325-3040 • www.cph.org

Manufactured in the United States of America

Library of Congress Cataloging-in-Publication Data

Rudnick, Milton L.
Journey into prayer / Milton L. Rudnick.
p. cm.
ISBN 978-0-7586-2380-5 (alk. paper)
1. Prayer--Christianity--Textbooks. I. Title.
BV214.R84 2010
248.3'2--dc22

2009053554

1 2 3 4 5 6 7 8 9 10 19 18 17 16 15 14 13 12 11 10

Contents

Introduction

Many of us realize that we have a long way to travel before our practice of prayer is what it ought to be. We do pray, of course, but our desire to pray is often weak and erratic. Our attention while praying is poor. The effect of our prayers seems uncertain. Disappointment and dissatisfaction follow our attempts to pray. Prayer does not do what we think it should, and we wonder if it means anything to God.

Jesus' disciples also felt the need to grow in prayer. Toward the end of His ministry, one of them approached Jesus with a straightforward request: "Lord, teach us to pray, as John taught his disciples" (Luke 11:1). There is no specific mention in the Gospels of John the Baptist doing this, but we are told that Peter and Andrew had been disciples of John before they began to follow Jesus (John 1:35). Part of what John had taught them was how to pray, but at this point they wanted to know more and be able to pray better.

It is not surprising that the disciples asked Jesus to help them. After all, He was the Messiah sent from heaven not only to save them but also to reveal all that they needed to know and do as His followers. Luke gives us some important background: "Now Jesus was praying in a certain place, and when He finished, one of His disciples said to Him, 'Lord, teach us to pray, as John taught his disciples' " (Luke 11:1). It was after observing Jesus in prayer, as they often did, that the disciples made this request.

JESUS PRAYED WITH AN UNEQUALED

FREQUENCY AND INTENSITY.

Jesus prayed with an unequaled frequency and intensity. Early in His ministry, as the first great crowds were drawn to His healing and preaching, we are told that He got up "very early in the morning, while it was still dark, [and] He departed and went out to a desolate place, and there He prayed" (Mark 1:35). Jesus often withdrew to a lonely place to pray (Luke 5:16), and even spent the entire night praying (Luke 6:12). In the Garden of Gethsemane on the night before He died, Jesus fell face down on the ground as He struggled in prayer with His Father about the terrible ordeal that was before Him (Matthew 26:39). To Jesus, prayer was central and essential. He prayed not because He had to or only to give a good example but because He needed it urgently. Sensing what prayer meant to Him and did for Him, one of the disciples longed for that experience and knew that the others felt the same way. All of this is behind the plea, "Lord, teach us to pray."

LORD, TEACH US TO PRAY.

Your Journey into Prayer

Think of this book as a journey into prayer, a venture that will take you closer to the prayer life that God wants you to have and that you realize you need. You will not be alone in this journey or alone as you study this book. God, through His Word and Spirit, will be your companion and mentor. It will be an interesting, exciting trip and much more. If you take this seriously and participate faithfully, you can expect to grow in both faith and prayer. God will cause you to grow. His purpose when He leads you into His Word is never just to inform or entertain. He means to change you. In the journey that you are about to begin, He is determined to turn you into the kind of person who will pray more eagerly, joyfully, and effectively than ever before.

For me, this study of prayer has become a personal journey. My long life as a Christian and long ministry as a pastor and professor has included much prayer. However, in recent years I have come to realize that there is still much more for me to discover and experience in prayer. As I moved further into prayer through the research and reflection required for this book, and as my practice of prayer has become more frequent and varied, the journey has become increasingly appealing and meaningful.

For more than thirteen years, my wife and I lived near the Rocky Mountains of Canada. During that time, we drove to Jasper and Banff National Parks and points in between more than twenty times, stopping along the way to absorb magnificent clusters of glacier-studded peaks cloaked with verdant forest, thundering waterfalls, emerald lakes, and awesome vistas. We can never get enough of that grandeur and beauty, and we have shared this spectacular part of God's creation with many family members and friends. Each time we make this same journey, we discover more to see and enjoy. Not long after each journey, the need and desire to do it again begins to grow, and we find ourselves looking forward to our next trip.

Prayer, too, is a journey to take over and over again. There is always more to learn—more joy, comfort, strength, and help to receive. Prayer is a form of communication, and like all communication, it has to be learned. We were not born ready to talk, read, and write. We had to learn through instruction, observation, trial and error, and practice. Prayer does not come naturally. It has to be learned by the long-term believer as well as the new believer. We all need to grow into it and keep growing.

Milton L. Rudnick

Roadblocks, Detours, and Wrong Turns

When you set off on a road trip during construction season, you can expect to encounter obstacles and delays. This journey into prayer is no exception. In fact, as we move toward a more active and meaningful prayer life, we may be more conscious of our problems in prayer than of anything else. It will be important and helpful to confront them at the beginning and prepare to deal with them. And we can do this confidently. It is neither right nor necessary for us to remain bogged down in our prayer problems and failures. We have no reason to be intimidated by them or to turn back because of them. Facing and understanding our problems in prayer with God's help will enable us to get through and past them to our destination.

In this chapter, we are going to explore and reflect on a variety of factors that can make prayer difficult for us or even discourage us from praying altogether. In later chapters, we will consider how these obstacles may be overcome. At this point we are simply diagnosing our condition; the treatment will follow another time.

Digging Deeper

1. How can roadblocks, detours, and wrong turns detract from a journey?

2. How might one respond to them?

Roadblocks to Prayer

If you are unable to start praying, what has gone wrong? If you have decided to spend special time in prayer, what thoughts and feelings can get in the way? One roadblock may be the suspicion that no one is listening, which will quickly kill the desire to pray. This may not be an expression of outright unbelief but a tragic misunderstanding instead. We may wrongly feel that God has so many more important things to take care of that there is no way He can or will pay attention to what we have to say. We may not reach this conclusion, but it remains a dark and unformed notion that can stop our prayer before we even get started.

Another such roadblock is the mistaken idea that prayer is not necessary. This idea often comes in the form of thinking that since

God already knows our needs and wants and has decided what He will do about them, there is no good reason to put our thoughts and wishes into prayer. This roadblock makes prayer seem unnecessary. It makes it appear that God is going to do what He wants anyway, so we are not in a position to influence Him; all we can do is go along with His wishes. We may take this to be the meaning of "Thy will be done," and thus have very little incentive to pray.

Still another obstacle that keeps us from prayer is the experience of unanswered prayer. We have often prayed that God would give us something or do something that was important to us, and it did not happen. So, we ask ourselves, "Why pray? Why get our hopes up only to have them dashed?" This way of thinking also forms a barrier that can frustrate and even kill our intention to pray.

"WHY PRAY?"

This book will address these and other similar issues. It is not difficult to recognize their source. Satan hates it when we pray. He intrudes into our thoughts whenever it is time to pray. His goal is to discourage us from praying or to turn prayer into something very different from what God intended. He is the one who tries to stop us on our journey into prayer.

Digging Deeper

1. Which of these roadblocks most often keep you from prayer?

2. What are some other roadblocks?

____

____

____

____

____

Detours on the Road to Prayer

There are many factors that slow us up, redirect us, and in other ways complicate our prayer journey.

Distractions are the most common detour on which we find ourselves. We are trying to concentrate on praying, and from within us or from our surroundings something draws us in a different direction. It may be that a prayer reminds us of something else, or an unexpected sound—such as the ringing of the telephone or footfalls in the hallway—makes our minds wander. Our focus on God and what we were going to say to Him is lost. It is like looking through binoculars at a distant object. After locating it, you steady your arms, make the object as large as possible, and carefully sharpen the focus. But then something jostles your arm, you lose the object, and only with some difficulty can you zero in on it again. Distractions interrupt our prayers by drawing our attention to other things.

DISTRACTIONS INTERRUPT OUR PRAYERS.

Inattentiveness is another kind of detour. Although we begin to pray, we may never get fully involved. Whether in church or in private, whether we are using a prepared or memorized prayer, we may be praying for one thing but thinking of another. Our participation is purely mechanical. Commenting on this kind of insincerity, God says, "This people draw near with their mouth and honor Me with their lips, while their hearts are far from Me" (Isaiah 29:13). Instead of directing our thoughts and words to God in prayer, we take them on a detour from which we often never return.

Procrastination also gets us off the track. Soon after we start or even before we begin to pray, we decide to put it off. We have to do something else. We are too busy or too tired. Another time will be better, but that time may never come. Such procrastination may grow out of laziness or be evidence of wrong priorities. It may reveal a lack of seriousness about the Lord, indifference to Him, or even a lack of concern about what is important to Him. A false sense of self-sufficiency can also be at the root of procrastination, the arrogant assumption that I really do not need to pray because I can take care of myself.

If Satan does not succeed in stopping us from praying altogether, he will strive to take our hearts and minds off prayer, or after we have begun, he will interrupt our prayer with the decision to postpone our prayers. We do not have to be deceived by Satan in these ways. Later lessons in this book will offer correctives for these detours.

Digging Deeper

1. Which of these detours do you take most often? What are some other detours not discussed here?

Wrong Turns

I once found myself driving around lost for an hour, several miles from home. The city was confusing because of the many twisting and frequently interrupted streets. But I had been there before and was looking for a destination I had recently visited. Studying the map did not help. I stopped and asked directions several times without success. After the trip, I studied the map one more time and found out what had happened. I had taken a wrong turn and left the freeway one exit too soon. Although I located the proper streets, they looked and acted differently than a mile down the road where I should have turned off the highway.

Few travel problems are more disconcerting than taking a wrong turn and not doing anything about it until you have gone a long distance in the wrong direction. On our journey into prayer, we can and do often take wrong turns whenever we turn prayer into something that it was never meant to be—when God's purpose for prayer is violated. Such wrong turns deprive us of the blessings God wants us to receive through prayer. We may think that we are offering valid prayers when, in fact, they are not prayers at all.

One such wrong turn is making prayer a bargaining session with God. "God, if You only give me what I want, I will do anything You ask. I will give up my favorite sins, go to church every Sunday, put more money in the offering envelope, and be nicer to my family." In other words, we approach prayer with the assumption we can buy what we want from God; we try to make a deal with Him that is so good He cannot refuse. God is very impatient and deeply offended with bargaining. It is a form of unbelief, a lack of confidence in His grace and love, as well as a sinful attempt to put Him in our debt. He not only ignores bargaining prayer, He condemns it.

GOD WANTS US TO PRAY IN JESUS' NAME.

The temptation to try to manipulate God through prayer is common, and it attempts to take a promise of God and force Him to do what we want. For example, Jesus says, "Therefore I tell you, whatever you ask in prayer, believe that you have received it, and it will be yours" (Mark 11:24). Three times in the Gospel of John, Jesus says that He or His Father will give us anything that we ask in His name (John 14:14; 15:16; 16:23). If we take these words seriously, we may insist: "Lord, I am praying in Your name, and I believe confidently that You will grant my request, so You have to do this. You have no choice." God wants us to pray in Jesus' name, and He wants us to take His promises seriously, but He does not want us to try to use them in such a way that we put ourselves in control.

Taking either of these wrong turns has frightening consequences. It puts us at odds with God and under His judgment. He does not take it lightly when we misuse prayer in these ways or others like them. In subsequent chapters we will consider how we can avoid wrong turns or recover from them.

Digging Deeper

1. Describe wrong turns we may take in our prayer journey.

2. Why are bargaining and manipulation distasteful to God?

Summary

As we set out on our journey into prayer, we can be certain that Satan will do everything possible to interfere. He will erect roadblocks and create detours. He will lead us into wrong turns—whatever it takes to discourage us or ruin our prayer. Something inside us is all too willing for this to happen. Our sinful nature is eager to avoid contact with God, to prevent, delay, or disrupt our journey into prayer. As much as this bothers Him, God does not give up on us. Through the sacrifice of Jesus, He offers us pardon for these sins that we commit in relation to prayer and keeps reaching out to us with His invitation and encouragement. He wants to keep the road open for this journey into prayer.

GOD DOES NOT GIVE UP ON US.

In the chapters that follow, we will make the most of the help that God has to offer. We will look carefully at:

1. what He says in His Word about prayer—what He means it to be;
2. the content of prayer—what we are to say;
3. listening to Him in prayer—making it a two-way conversation;
4. God's response to prayer—how He feels about it and reacts to it;
5. arrangements—where, when, and how to pray;
6. resources for prayer—where to find beautiful and meaningful prayers from the experience of other believers;
7. prayer companions—partners, groups, and chains; and
8. the never-ending journey—prayer.

Learning by Doing

A helpful way to grow in prayer is to pray together with other believers. This should be done in a sensitive and nonthreatening way and in a way that will gradually help everyone participating to become more comfortable praying aloud, from the heart, and in the presence of others. If there is anything that many of us need to improve, this is it.

PRAY TOGETHER

WITH OTHER BELIEVERS.

If you are studying this book in a group, begin with a simple form of group prayer. After a brief introductory prayer by one member, others are invited to offer brief, specific requests (intercessions) and special thanks to the Lord to which the group offers an appropriate response. You may wish to begin with requests and follow with thanksgivings. Your personal prayer may follow the same pattern. Examples:

Requests: "Healing for Mary," "A job for Joe," or "Peace in the Middle East . . . "

After each request (all) say, "Lord, hear our prayer."

Thanksgiving: "For rain," "For reconciliation with a loved one," or "For a new grandchild . . . "

After each thanksgiving (all) say, "We thank You, Lord."

When all requests and thanksgivings have been offered, someone offers a brief conclusion to which all respond, "Amen."

Notes

The Destination

Our journey has a destination. We are going somewhere important, to be with someone to whom we need to talk. For many of us, our favorite trip is a visit with friends or family. We look forward to spending time with them, and we prepare ourselves mentally and emotionally. The people we are visiting are the big attraction. Any activities and entertainment are secondary. Prayer takes us to God, and we want to make the most of this meeting with Him.

PRAYER TAKES US TO GOD.

The Purpose: Communication

As we move toward our destination, we anticipate it as an opportunity for a privileged and unique form of communication. This is not simply small talk; it is entry into the heart and mind of another person, someone who already knows us better than anyone else, who loves us more than anyone else, and who responds to us with the utmost generosity and power. This is the most personal and important communication in which we can engage.

Prayer is such a familiar part of our lives that we often take it for granted or tragically underappreciate it. What a mistake! An opportunity to communicate with the God of heaven and earth, the Creator of everything, should not be taken for granted. We are approaching the One who laid down His life so that we could escape the terrible fate that our sins brought upon us, the One who made us eligible to enter the presence of His Father. Our prayer is so important to God that He facilitates it with the presence and support of His Spirit (Romans 8:26–27).

When we reach out to God in prayer, we always make immediate personal contact. We are heading toward a personal meeting with our God, who guarantees His full attention and His loving understanding. He anticipates our conversation and will welcome us with open arms. He is ready and willing to hear whatever we have to say. In fact, before we ever address Him, He tunes into our thoughts and feelings, gets involved in our lives behind the scenes, and is just waiting for us to notice Him and speak to Him. That is how seriously He takes us. That is how much we mean to Him.

Digging Deeper

1. Describe an experience in which you tried unsuccessfully to talk either in person or on the phone to some busy and important person—a high-level public official, a customer service supervisor, or a celebrity.

2. How does communication technology affect personal communication—positively and negatively?

3. What does it take to get in touch with God?

____

____

____

____

____

Ultrapersonal Communication

The way you talk (or not talk) to someone is determined largely by the nature of your relationship. If the person is someone whom you know very well, love, respect, and feel comfortable with, your conversation will be warm and intimate. If the person is a stranger, you will be more guarded in what you say and may not wish to say anything at all. Your words to a young child will be of one kind if it is your own child, but quite different if it is a child that you do not even know. Relationships have a profound effect on communication. Prayer is communication within the most important relationship that any of us have, our relationship with God.

God wants our relationship with Him to be close and personal, and the Bible expresses this. In many passages He refers to our relationship with Him as that of children to their father. That term can be problematic for some who have had human fathers who are aloof, mean, thoughtless, or even cruel. However, God makes it clear in Scripture that He is different from an uncaring earthly father. He reminds His Old Testament people that He carried them as a father carries his son (Deuteronomy 1:31). Picture a father and son trudging through a barren wilderness, exhausted. When the son gives out, the father lifts the boy to his shoulders and, without regard to his own comfort and well-being, carries him to safety. Elsewhere, God refers to Himself as the Father who created us (Malachi

2:10); a compassionate Father (Psalm 103:13); a Father who corrects us lovingly as children in whom He delights (Proverbs 3:12). Jesus emphatically relates all this to prayer. When the disciples asked Him to teach them to pray, He told them to address God as "Our Father in heaven" (Matthew 6:9). Prayer is communication within the warmth, trust, and intimacy of a relationship with our loving Father in heaven. What could be more inviting?

PRAYER IS COMMUNICATION WITH

OUR LOVING FATHER IN HEAVEN.

God further enriches our view of our relationship with Him by comparing it with that of a mother and a nursing infant. "You shall nurse, you shall be carried upon her hip, and bounced upon her knees. As one whom his mother comforts, so I will comfort you" (Isaiah 66:12b–13a). The tenderness of that scene is a tremendous encouragement to pray. The infant is hungry, afraid, in pain, and in need. The mother is alert to every cry and whimper and will hold the child close, console, and soothe with words and caresses that no substitute can duplicate. Likewise, God responds when we cry out to Him in our need.

God also pictures Himself as the husband of His people. "For your Maker is your husband," the prophet Isaiah says (54:5), and in Jeremiah the Lord says, "For I am your husband" (3:14 NIV). St. Paul says to those whom he brought to faith, "I betrothed you to one husband . . . Christ" (2 Corinthians 11:2), and he portrays Christ as a loving sacrificial husband to the Church, which is His Body (Ephesians 5:25–33). Even in a culture that emphasizes their equality and independence, many women look for the kind of husband who loves them unselfishly, provides for them, protects them, and, above all, listens to them. That is the kind of husband God is.

He is not only willing to listen, He also is eager for us to share whatever is in our hearts and minds. He seeks the kind of ultrapersonal communication that can be found in only the healthiest marriages.

God also uses the metaphor of friendship to help us to grasp the kind of relationship and communication He hopes to have with us. Abraham is described as God's friend (James 2:23), and God's relationship and communication with Moses is given as a model of what God wants to have with all of us. "Thus the Lord used to speak to Moses face to face, as a man speaks to his friend" (Exodus 33:11), and it is clear that Moses spoke to God in the same way (Exodus 32:11–14). Jesus addresses His followers as His friends to whom He reveals everything and for whom He would exercise love in the extreme, the kind that lays down His life for His friends (John 15:12–17). Many of us have human friends with whom we long to communicate on a regular basis and to whom we can tell anything, even after many years of separation. Jesus says that this is the kind of friendship and sharing we can have with Him. Prayer is a priceless opportunity to experience this friendship.

Digging Deeper

1. What are some qualities of a relationship that encourage communication, and which of these are most prominent in our relationship with God?

2. What are factors that prevent good communication with God or other people, and what can be done about them?

____

____

____

____

____

Factors That Enhance Relational Communication

Relationships require and thrive on good communication—primarily verbal communication. For this reason, God lovingly encourages and invites us to communicate with Him in prayer. Our faith relationship is as important to Him as it is to us, not because He needs us, but because He loves us. He created us for that relationship. Jesus laid down His life to make up for all that makes us unworthy of God. The Holy Spirit continually enables us to make the most of that relationship. He wants that relationship to grow to the point that God is more important than anything else, and this can happen as we reach out to Him with words of prayer. Of course there are also important and effective nonverbal forms of communication. A facial expression, tone of voice, gesture, touch, or gift can all convey important meaning. But, above all, personal communication consists of thoughts and feelings expressed in words. Prayer is that kind of communication.

Good communication is open and honest, and this is what God seeks from us. We have every reason to pray that way because He reads our thoughts and hearts anyway. In addition, our prayer means more to us, as well as to Him, when we hold nothing back. Furthermore, our communication with God is enriched when we give it priority, when we faithfully and lovingly withdraw so that we can concentrate solely on Him as Jesus did, and when we are willing to devote the time and attention necessary to nurture our relationship with Him in prayer.

Summary

It is both humbling and thrilling to realize that God sincerely longs to hear from us and that our relationship means so much to Him. In Psalm 62:8, He tells us that we should pour out our hearts to Him because He is our refuge. Jesus says that we should love God with all our heart, soul, mind, and strength (Mark 12:30), and prayer is the language of that love. Often, people have no time for or any interest in us. We may approach them hoping to unburden ourselves to them or at least to be in their company, but their minds are on other things or they have other plans. God, on the other hand, is always available, interested, and even eager to hear from us and to share our lives. No problem, hurt, or joy is too small to engage His attention. No temptation, sin, or doubt is so great that we cannot confidently bring it to Him.

Digging Deeper

1. How would you feel if someone you loved failed to return your phone calls or invitations or would not pay attention to your conversation?

____

____

____

____

____

2. How do frequent, intimate, and leisurely conversations strengthen relationships?

Learning by Doing

In your prayer time, use the same simple form that was recommended in the previous chapter.

1. After an introductory statement to the Lord, first offer intercessions (requests), and respond with, "Lord, hear our (my) prayer."
2. Next offer thanksgivings, and respond with, "We (I) thank You, Lord."
3. After a summary statement to the Lord, conclude with "Amen."

Whether you are praying privately or in a group, do not be in a hurry. Allow some time to formulate the intercessions and thanksgivings.

Notes

3

The Itinerary

Conversation is often like a journey. It moves in one direction for a while and then turns in a different direction as participants shift from topic to topic. In this chapter, we explore the course of our conversation with God that we call "prayer."

What is conversation like between loved ones and dear friends? What do you talk about? You may begin with some ordinary and mundane matters—sports, politics, even the weather. But, if the conversation is truly meaningful, if it touches you deeply and enriches your relationship, you will move beyond the superficial to areas of major significance. It is an experience in which you open your hearts to one another and share the contents with love and trust. Prayer is meant to be that kind of communication between you and God. When we approach prayer or are at prayer, this is the kind of conversation for which we ought to strive.

In this chapter, we are considering only our side of the conversation. We want to set the direction of our prayers with God, what we could and should be saying to Him, and the way God hopes the conversation will develop. Usually when we prepare for an important conversation, we give thought to the direction that we hope it will take. Prayer is the most important conversation in which we engage. In the next chapter we will look at God's side of the conversation—how He speaks to us in connection with prayer. In this chapter, we will reflect only on what we will say to Him.

PRAYER IS THE MOST IMPORTANT

CONVERSATION IN WHICH WE ENGAGE.

Whom Do We Address?

While conversing with several persons, it is important to know whom you should address—to all equally or primarily to one? God has revealed Himself in Scripture as a triune being, tri-personal and yet just one God. To which person do we talk in prayer? Father, Son, and Holy Spirit are each wholly and completely God, and yet each has a distinct personality. They are so distinct that they speak to one another. Each has a distinct part to play in the work of salvation—the Father creates, the Son redeems, and the Holy Spirit sanctifies—as well as a different relationship with the other two. This does not mean that we have three Gods. The Bible reminds us repeatedly that God is one, and only one, divine being (Mark 12:29, 32). The persons of the Godhead are distinct but not separate. We can tell them apart, but they do not come apart. We could say that 1+1+1=1. While this is not good arithmetic, it is a helpful way to state the mysterious complexity of our God. Each of us is just one person. Our one God is three. It should not surprise us that God is more complicated than we are.

All this causes us to ask: whom do we address in prayer? In the majority of the prayers recorded in Scripture, God the Father is addressed, and this is how Jesus taught us to pray. However, Jesus also specifically invites us to pray to Him (John 14:14), and prayer is often addressed to Him (Acts 7:59; 22:10; Hebrews 4:14–16; Revelation 5:6–14). Research for this chapter revealed no scriptural prayer addressed to the Holy Spirit. However, because He is also true God, Christians from all ages have also addressed the Holy Spirit in prayer. There are a number of beautiful hymns in which prayer is offered to the Holy Spirit. Check your hymnal index for examples.

Since each person of the Trinity is true God and therefore worthy, available, and interested in hearing from us, and since each is also fully capable of responding to our prayers, it is appropriate to address any of the three. Because they are completely united, we can be sure that prayer addressed to one reaches the entire Godhead.

Christian practice reflects the emphasis of the Bible. Ordinarily we address our prayer to God the Father. However, prayers are most complete when they acknowledge all three persons. Jesus tells us to pray in His name (John 14:13; 16:24). Only He and what He did for us on the cross gives us access to the Father. So, to pray in His name means to ask God to hear us for Jesus' sake. St. Paul explains that the Holy Spirit is our helper in prayer. Often, we hardly know what to pray for or cannot even get started, and when that happens the Holy Spirit prays for us and with us (Romans 8:26–27). These truths shape our prayers. We pray to the Father through the Son with the help of the Holy Spirit. Our prayers may appropriately include a request to the Holy Spirit for His help as well as admission to the Father that we do not deserve His attention and help. Yet we ought to ask God the Father for His help and attention because His Son earned this right for us and promised that we would be heard.

Digging Deeper

1. Does the fact that God is three persons make communication with Him more or less personal than if He were only one person?

____

____

____

____

2. What kind of prayers do you feel are most appropriately offered to the Father? the Son? the Holy Spirit?

Into the Heart of God

In the Lord's Prayer (Matthew 6:5–15), Jesus teaches that our prayer conversation with God should first lead us into God's heart, into things that matter most to Him. We should give attention to His priorities, purposes, hopes, dreams, and promises. He tells us this in the petitions: "Hallowed be Your name. Your kingdom come, Your will be done, on earth as it is in heaven." This is where God's heart is, and this is where He would like us to begin when we pray—with the people and events that bring Him honor, with that which extends His influence over us and in the world, and with whatever makes people able and willing to do His will. He wants us to pray about these things so that we experience our partnership with Him in His great work. This short list—His name, His influence, and His will—does not exhaust the content of God's heart, but it does make the point that this is where we should begin in prayer, the first stop on our prayer journey. However, it is not the end of our journey. After we have visited His heart, God gently turns us in a different direction.

Into Our Own Hearts and Lives

In prayer, God also wants us to enter into our own hearts and lives so that we can share what is there. Jesus brings this out in the last four petitions of the Lord's Prayer, which teach us to speak to Him about our most urgent material and spiritual needs. Daily bread includes not only food but also everything that we need for this body and life. Forgiveness is our most basic spiritual need. Until and unless we are forgiven through Jesus' blood and death, we cannot expect any other good thing from God. Strength against temptation is vital if we hope to improve and grow in our relationship with Him. Deliverance from Satan (evil) is protection against the devil's schemes and actions that are designed to destroy us. God has planted the desire for strength and deliverance in our hearts. He wants us to take these desires seriously and talk to Him about them. They are representative of the entire range of help from God that we need and want.

In fact, He wants us to share everything in our hearts and minds—every concern, every hurt, and every failure, as well as every joy, every success, every hope, and every dream. Sometimes we think that He is interested in hearing only about matters of supreme importance and that we should not bother God with the little things of life. But this is not the case at all. If it is important to us, or even seems important, He hopes that we will tell Him about it. God's love for us is so large and strong that He is interested in everything about us. And, of course, it is not that He needs the information. He knows what is going on in our lives without our reporting it, but He likes to hear from us. He loves it when we think of Him and want to be in touch with Him. The sound of our voice and the attitude of our hearts are more important to Him than any thoughts, words, and feelings that we might send His way. Isn't this true of communication with anyone to whom you are close? Often the content of the conversation includes nothing new, but the words exchanged nurture the relationship just the same.

Digging Deeper

1. Why does God ask us to give priority in prayer to His concerns?

2. Do you ever hesitate to pray about the little things of life? Why?

Into the Problems and Needs of Others

After entering into God's heart and then into our own, the itinerary of our conversation moves in a new direction. We turn from our personal concerns and God's concerns to those of other people. This part of prayer is called "intercession"—speaking to God in behalf of others. The better we get to know other people, if we are at all perceptive, the more conscious we become of their problems and needs. Their material or temporal needs might be for healing, comfort, recovery from addiction, reconciliation in a broken relationship, money, or better grades. Their spiritual needs might include saving faith, deliverance from doubt or despair, trust in God's promises, repentance, hope, or faithfulness. In addition to the problems and needs of those whom we know from personal contact, there are many others that we only hear or read about. Everyone has these kinds of needs. God wants us to be aware of them and concerned about them, and He wants us to bring them before Him in prayer.

Digging Deeper

1. How can we become more aware of the needs of others and be sure to remember them in prayer?

2. How long should we keep praying for others?

3. How bold and specific should we be in our intercessions for others?

Back to God in Thanksgiving and Praise

After first entering God's own heart, then ours, then the problems and needs of others, the course of our prayer conversation comes right back to God. As we reflect on the high privilege that is ours in prayer, that the God of the universe is interested in us and our prayers, that He highly values communicating with us, and that He even loves to grant our requests, we are moved to deep gratitude and heartfelt praise. Thanksgiving is our response to what He gives and does. Praise is admiration for who He is. Thanksgiving and praise focus on Him, His goodness, His wisdom, His power, and His mercy. Thanksgiving is appreciation. Praise is adoration. Although thanksgiving and praise are distinct elements of prayer, they are so closely related that they are often intermingled. The most vivid and powerful scenes of thanksgiving and adoration recorded in the Bible are found in Revelation 4, 5, and 7, which describe the way thanksgiving and adoration are done in heaven.

Digging Deeper

1. Why does God want our praise and thanksgiving?

2. Why are thanksgiving and praise offered to God important to us?

Staying on Course—Persistence in Prayer

It is easy to misunderstand God's intentions regarding our prayer. If we pray for something repeatedly and nothing seems to happen, we assume that God's answer is no. This makes us want to give up, to quit asking, and to drop out of the conversation. After all, this is what it would mean if we consistently failed to grant a request. Although we might not put it into words, we would hope the petitioner would get the message: "I am not going to do it so please quit bothering me."

However, that is not what God is trying to convey in such a situation. Although He does not seem to be responding, He wants us to be persistent in prayer. God likes it when we pray. He loves to hear from us, especially when we keep asking for the same thing. He means to draw out our faith. We learn this from the experience of the woman with a demon-possessed daughter. When she first pleaded with Jesus to heal her daughter, He did not even answer her. But that did not discourage her. She sensed that He really cared and wanted to grant her request. Even though she asked two more times and received discouraging replies, she kept at it, and eventually Jesus was happy to grant her request and praised her for her faith (Matthew 15:21–28).

Jesus told the parable of the persistent widow who tried to get a judge to deal with a grievance. He did not fear God or care about her, but because she kept pestering him, the judge finally relented. Imagine, Jesus says, if that kind of person will finally be moved by persistence, how much more will your loving and generous heavenly Father be moved by your persistent prayer requests (Luke 18:1–8). So, stay the course. Keep praying confidently and tenaciously. Do not drop out. Many Christians report that they prayed for years, even decades, before God finally granted their request. Their reaction to this was not disappointment or bitterness. Rather, they realized that all this praying benefited them and their relationship with God. Furthermore, when the request was finally granted, it meant more to them than if they had received it immediately.

KEEP PRAYING CONFIDENTLY AND TENACIOUSLY.

A handsome, gleaming, white church towers over the village of Toksovo, which is located about fifteen miles northeast of St. Petersburg, Russia. While there for a church conference I met a woman with a story of courageous and persistent prayer. She told me her story through an interpreter who verified its accuracy. This is what she said as we stood outside admiring the elegant place of worship:

> I was baptized in this church as a baby and confirmed there as a young woman. But then the Communists took our pastors away to prison, and we never saw them again. Next, they took the cross from the steeple, removed all Christian symbols and pictures from the inside, and turned it into a dance hall. It broke my heart, but I didn't give up. Every day for sixty years I stood in front of that building and prayed that God would return it to us.
>
> People from the village ridiculed me by saying that my prayers would not change anything, and besides, they needed it for a dance hall.

Then, turning her eyes toward the building and with her face radiant, she continued:

> And look how wonderfully God has answered my prayers. The church has been restored with money from Finland. A congregation of one thousand members gathers here, and today pastors and delegates from all over Russia are here doing the Lord's work!

Digging Deeper

1. What are some temptations that we face when God does not seem to be granting our requests?

____

____

____

____

____

2. Describe an answered prayer and the ways God granted more than you had even asked.

____

____

____

____

____

Summary

Often a major obstacle or inhibition that prevents us from praying, either in private or in a group, is that we do not know what to say. This chapter suggests a simple but helpful agenda, an itinerary for our journey into prayer, which in every situation will help us know what needs to be said. When you pray, say:

1. *I am sorry!* Confess your sins as they relate to the day or the situation.
2. *Help!* Ask for God's assistance and intervention in the things that are important to Him, to you, and to others.

3. *Thanks!* Itemize and express appreciation for His many gifts.
4. *Praise!* Tell Him how much you admire and honor Him for who He is.

Learn by Doing

In private or in a group, offer prayer about your prayer life and the specific issues addressed in this chapter. You will find it helpful to use the four points listed above.

Notes

4

Two-Way Traffic

One-way streets may be advantageous on the road, but this is not the case in the journey of prayer. Prayer is communication, a very special conversation between you and God. You have spoken with people who insist on doing all the talking and have no real interest in what you have to say. A one-way conversation is really no conversation at all.

We need to listen to God—carefully. Until we listen, we are not able or ready to speak to Him. He wants to be an active conversational partner. The most complete and effective prayer is what we are saying in response to what God says to us. This chapter is a discussion of how God does—and does not—speak to us in prayer.

God's Communication Media

Although the Bible relates God speaking to someone in a dream, vision, or through some other unusual event, these are not His usual ways of communicating with people. Most often, God spoke in less spectacular ways—through other people such as prophets and apostles, through His written Word, as well as through simple acts connected with His Word—Baptism and the Lord's Supper.

When we are seeking comfort, guidance, or even correction, we wish God would speak to us loudly and clearly. We wish He would do something to convey His response in an unmistakable manner. This desire is so strong in some Christians that they convince themselves and others that they have heard such messages and seen such signs, though this may not have happened at all. Jesus expressed serious disappointment in those who insist on seeing signs and wonders and other tangible evidence before they accept Him or the message about Him (John 4:48; 20:29).

We must grant that God can communicate in any way He chooses and that He may still use these unusual methods. However, we must also realize that they are rare exceptions and that He does not need to use them to communicate with us effectively. We should gratefully and confidently listen to Him through the means He ordinarily likes to employ. We call these "the Means of Grace" because through them God reaches out to us with the grace that we need so desperately—the grace that includes both His forgiveness and the strength of His Holy Spirit.

Digging Deeper

1. God expresses His love and His will for us in several different ways. What are some ways in which you express your wishes and feelings for someone?

2. How are the ways you express yourself to others similar to God's ways? How are they different?

The Message Within

When we pray, in a sense, God speaks to us through what is already in our hearts and minds. The conversational traffic flows in both directions. We speak to Him in prayer, and He responds through His Word that has been planted (James 1:21) and is living and growing within us (Colossians 3:16). This does not mean that we can make up what we want to hear from God and then convince ourselves that it comes from Him. No, it means that when we hear or read His Word or receive it in sacramental form, His Word sends down roots and becomes a living, growing, lasting source of revelation and direction for us. God's Word is present and powerful not only at the time we receive it from the Scriptures or the Sacraments, but also as it continues to remain active, influential, and empowering within us. "But the word is very near you. It is in your mouth and in your heart" (Deuteronomy 30:14). God's Word becomes part of us. It is ready to speak to us whenever we remember or reflect on it, and it can affect us quietly and inconspicuously even when we are not aware of it.

GOD'S WORD IS PRESENT AND POWERFUL.

The significance of this greatly affects our prayer experience. Understand that when we pray, we are neither talking to ourselves nor doing all the talking. We are interacting with God. The Holy Spirit is present in person when we pray and actively responds to us through His implanted Word. When we are praying about a difficult moral decision, a temptation, an urgent personal need—whatever—we can recall what God has said about this in His Word and let it speak to our situation. If we cannot remember, we can ask God to bring it to mind, help us to find it in the Bible, or direct us to someone who can lead us to it. God is eager to share His plans, thoughts, and feelings with us. It is as important to Him as it is to us that prayer be a two-way conversation. No one who wants to hear from God will be met with silence for long.

All of this emphasizes the importance of a continuous intake of God's Word, of hearing, reading, and studying it frequently. Prayer begins with God talking to us, and it is sustained as we keep listening to Him. Through His Word, God gives us His Holy Spirit who becomes active in us. His purpose is not only to bring us information about God but also to enable us to know God in a meaningful, personal way so that our relationship with Him becomes richer and stronger. When that happens, God's thoughts, desires, and emotions become more our own, and our character and behavior are shaped increasingly into His image. Then, when we pray, we almost instinctively know God's plan, attitude, and will about what is on our hearts and minds. He speaks to us through this transforming influence of His Spirit in the implanted Word.

Digging Deeper

1. Do you ever know or "hear" what someone is saying to you even when he or she is not with you or speaking directly to you? How does this happen?

2. Think of cases in which you have listened to God in an apparently instinctive manner.

The Importance of Good Listening

Whether it comes to us from hearing, reading, or the influence of what has been implanted within, God's Word will not register and will not benefit us unless we are fully attentive to it—unless we really listen, understand, and take it to heart. God's Word does not work mechanically and automatically like the oxygen we breathe that keeps us alive and healthy without our notice.

God's Word is a personal communication that requires awareness, interest, and understanding on our part. He wants us to become fully involved in His part of the prayer conversation. God wants us to take Him and His Word seriously. The Holy Spirit performs His miracles of faith, transformation, and deliverance upon those with open ears and minds. In reference to the way that God's Word works on people, Jesus says, "He who has ears, let him hear" (Matthew 13:9). Therefore, when we open our Bibles or hear a sermon, we must listen intently to what God is telling us so that it can connect with us and help us. It also means that when we are praying, we must frequently shift our focus away from what we want, need, or worry about to God so His Word can get through to us.

Much of our prayer is problem centered. When we focus on what is wrong, the problems seem enormous and unsolvable, and it is depressing. Or, we are all wrapped up in our selfish interests or desires, which leaves us feeling deprived or frustrated. When we focus on God and absorb His truth and promises, we realize that He is greater and wiser than anything that is bothering us, and this brings us joy and hope. When we focus on His incomparable love and generosity, we are assured that our prayers will always be answered in the way that is best for us. If different from what we wanted, we have no reason to be disappointed. We can only be relieved and grateful to know that God always influences the course of our lives and the world in ways that will benefit us (Romans 8:28).

LISTEN CAREFULLY TO GOD'S WORD.

We are told repeatedly in Scripture to listen carefully to God's Word. In the parable of the sower, Jesus compares a good listener to good soil in which seed can spring up, grow, and produce fruit (Matthew 13:1–23). It is only by a miracle of the Holy Spirit that we can believe and be saved, but we are already equipped to listen to God and take His Word seriously. Good listening enables God's Word to become a strong and productive influence within us. When Mary listened to Jesus' Word while her sister was busy fixing a meal for Him, Jesus made it clear that Mary had her priorities straight (Luke 10:38–42). After referring to Himself as the Good Shepherd, Jesus explained that we, His sheep, are to listen to His voice and follow Him (John 10:27). James tells us to be quick to listen and slow to speak (James 1:19). This is important to keep in mind with regard to prayer. Our prayers are most effective and uplifting when they grow out of good listening to God's Word.

Digging Deeper

1. Why is good listening in prayer so important?

____

____

____

____

2. What interferes with our listening to God?

____

____

____

____

Acknowledging and Dealing with Failure

When we cannot seem to hear God, when His side of the conversation seems silent, the fault is not His. He is there, and He is speaking. The problem is that we are not really listening. We may be saying something to Him, but we are self-centered, not focusing on God's response. In fact, we may hardly even be conscious of His presence and His involvement in the conversation. Like the tiresome and insensitive person who monopolizes every conversation, we prevent God from getting a word in edgewise.

This offends and disappoints God. He has much to say to us that we need, and we owe Him our full attention. He loves us intensely and wants to open His heart to us. He wants to help us understand Him better, realize more clearly what we are facing in life, and know confidently how we should respond. Above all, He wants to be closer and more important to us, and this can happen only if, when we pray, we truly focus on Him. When our minds wander, our awareness of Him fades or our prayer degenerates into hypocritical listening, God reacts with anger and disgust. He offers us His presence and loving attention, and we carelessly tune Him out.

Summary

We need to recognize our failure to listen, to confess this sin that we so often commit while praying, and then to listen with faith to His word of forgiveness, which we have heard and read so often. The Holy Spirit reminds us of the message of pardon through Jesus' suffering whenever we confess our sins to God. And, when we receive that forgiveness, we also receive the help and strength we need to listen more carefully in the future. It is as important to listen to God as it is to talk to Him. Unless the traffic of our prayer conversation goes in both directions, it is not prayer at all.

Digging Deeper

1. How would you feel if your conversation partner was not listening to you?

2. What are some Bible passages that help us become more aware of God's presence when we pray and more open to what He has to say?

3. What are some statements that assure us of God's pardon when we are sorry for our sins?

Learning by Doing

In private or in a group, offer a prayer about listening to God while praying. Follow the four categories discussed in the previous chapter, and expand them to fit your situation.

1. *I am sorry*, Lord, for not listening (give details). Forgive me because of Jesus' death on my behalf.

2. *Help me* to give my full attention to You while praying and to listen to Your implanted Word.
3. *Thanks* for the high privilege of knowing You and entering Your presence.
4. *I praise You,* for You are wonderful, able, and eager to be in conversation with me.

Notes

5

A Life-Changing Journey

A young man from the Midwest traveled to California for a family gathering, and it changed his life. While there, he accepted a job offer at which he proved to be extraordinarily successful. Alone, he joined a young adult Bible study group and became more serious about his faith. Neighbors in his condominium complex introduced him to the woman he soon married. They have three children and are very happy—all because he took that journey.

Our journey into prayer can be that kind of journey. It can change everything. As we take the opportunity to move forward in our prayer life, take prayer more seriously, and make it more meaningful and effective, we can expect some major differences to take place, not only in us personally but also in others around us and even in the world. Prayer has that effect.

Digging Deeper

1. What are some changes that you hope will be brought about through prayer?

2. What are some changes that God would like to bring about through prayer?

____

____

____

____

____

The God Who Changes Things

God answers prayer. He promised this. He is committed to it, and He does it. Jesus said, "Whatever you ask in My name, this I will do, that the Father may be glorified in the Son. If you ask Me anything in My name, I will do it" (John 14:13–14). Many believers have experienced exactly what Jesus is talking about here.

God is an interested, responsive, and active listener. God is profoundly interested in us and in everything that we say to Him in prayer. He gives everyone who prays His full attention, even while millions are praying at the same time. Furthermore, He not only listens to our words, but He also searches our minds and hearts while we pray so that He has a complete and accurate understanding of what we say (Psalm 139:1–4). No one else can listen with that kind of love, interest, and insight.

As mentioned in the previous chapter, God also enters into the conversation. He speaks to you as you speak to Him. Through the Holy Spirit in the Word implanted within you, God brings to mind what you have heard and read from Scripture that relates to the things about which you are praying. Whether you are praying about your fears or worries, hopes or dreams, guilt or discouragement, happiness or health, loneliness or sorrow, loved ones or enemies, prosperity or poverty, temptations or victories, ask yourself, "What has God told me about this in His Word? What has He done about such things? How does He feel about them?"

Look in your Bible, especially in the Psalms, and you will not look far before finding something that addresses your situation or concerns. Obviously, the more you study the Bible and absorb its contents, the more readily God will be able to speak to you in prayer. In almost every sermon there is truth or guidance of some kind that comes through clearly and helpfully, whether you need it now or in the future. When you hear it, make a note in which you summarize that point in one sentence and give the Bible text on which it is based. Reflect on this point until it is part of you. Then, when you are praying and need it, God will speak to you through His Word.

GOD WILL SPEAK TO YOU THROUGH HIS WORD.

Prayer becomes most meaningful and effective when, as we pray, we listen attentively to God. Instead of being just a list of things that we want to say, prayer becomes a lively conversation in which we are stimulated and enriched by input from our God.

God is an active listener. When we tell Him what is bothering us or what we need or want, He does not simply lend a sympathetic ear. He does something about it. He takes delight in granting our requests, and no request is too much for Him. He is as powerful as He is creative and resourceful. He likes to make changes that are important to us. If He does not seem to do or give what we ask, His answer may not be no, but rather later. His sense of timing is perfect. He always acts when it will do the most good. Or, when He seems to be denying our request, He may have revised our request. If He does not give us what we want, we do not go away empty-handed. Rather, we get something even better. St. Paul prayed earnestly and repeatedly that God would deliver him from his "thorn in the flesh," a painful and disabling illness, but instead God gave him a marvelous experience of sustaining grace, which Paul valued above the healing for which he had pleaded (2 Corinthians 12:7–10).

Digging Deeper

1. Why is it sometimes difficult to realize that God is such an interested, responsive, and active listener?

   ____

   ____

   ____

   ____

2. Have you or someone you know ever received something better from God than what was requested?

   ____

   ____

   ____

   ____

Seek and Expect Bold and Specific Changes

On the one hand, we do not make demands of God in prayer because, after all, He is God. We gladly accept His answer to our prayers because we trust Him and know His way is always best. On the other hand, He invites us to be very bold and specific in our prayer requests, assuring us that He can change anything and that He likes to answer prayer with dramatic, even miraculous, changes. Jesus said that if, in faith, we ask God to pick up a mountain and throw it into the sea, He can and will do that (Mark 11:22–24).

From what Jesus says elsewhere, we understand that He will do such things if our situation requires it and it will best serve our interests. After all, God parted the Red Sea so that His people could escape their enemies (Exodus 14). Jesus stopped a life-threatening storm with a word of command (Mark 4:35–41) and healed large numbers of sick people upon request (Mark 1:29–34). All this encourages us to be very bold and specific in our prayers.

BE BOLD AND SPECIFIC IN PRAYER.

Often our prayers are vague and timid. We hesitate to tell God exactly what we would like Him to do, especially if it involves something very big, dramatic, or miraculous. We may think that such a request would be presumptuous. Or, we may doubt that He would do it anyway, and we do not want to be disappointed. Therefore, our prayers remain very general and modest. For example, "Lord, give me strength to bear this burden and always to know that I am safe in Your hands no matter what happens." This is a very good and appropriate prayer, and there are times when this is all we need to say. However, Jesus also encourages us to present enormous and definite requests.

My personal experience bears this out. On one occasion I was rushed to the hospital in an ambulance because I was at serious risk for a heart attack. An echocardiogram had revealed a calcified valve, and I had developed chest pains. In addition, my father had died from a heart attack. The doctor said that I would probably require either a replacement valve, angioplasty to clear the arteries, or both. My prayers and those of others who prayed for me were similar to the one in the previous paragraph. However, one of my friends was very bold and specific, saying, "Lord, what we need for this brother is healing. We are asking You to make that valve function properly and clear those arteries so that he can resume his life and ministry unimpaired." After another echocardiogram and an angiogram that explored the arteries, the doctor gave me his report. Although the valve was still calcified, it was functioning normally—as was the entire organ. Furthermore, the arteries were clear. I was released from the hospital with no restrictions. Was this just a coincidence, or was it the answer to a bold and specific prayer? I cannot prove it, but I know what I believe.

There is more. I mentioned my experience to a Bible study group. The next week one of the class members came to me radiant with joy about an answer to his prayer. He and his wife had been trying to adopt another child for several years, and nothing was happening. "I remembered what you said about prayer," he explained. "I was driving in my car, holding a cold drink, when I realized that I should pray very directly about the adoption. All I said was, 'Lord, we want a child now!' and was so excited about that prayer that I spilled my drink. When I got home, my wife greeted me with the good news. 'They have a child for us. We can pick him up next week.' "

Such experiences can always be explained away; there is no conclusive scientific proof for them. However, in view of our God and His amazing invitation to pray this way, faith sees nothing in such experiences but God acting powerfully and decisively to answer prayer.

Digging Deeper

1. What is the boldest and most specific request you ever made in prayer?

2. What is the most dramatic answer to prayer that you ever received or heard about?

____

____

____

____

____

The Most Important Change

"Prayer changes things. Prayer changes you!" This familiar Christian saying has been around for a long time, and it expresses a very important truth. No change that God works in answer to prayer is more important than the change He brings about in the heart and life of the one who prays. Hopefully, many of our prayers will include requests that God make such changes. However, even when such requests are not included, prayer changes us.

The more we seriously and attentively pray, the more we will be aware of God. If as we go about our daily lives and if we enter into conversation with God about what we are planning, doing, and struggling with, our consciousness of God and His involvement in our life will grow tremendously. We will be living in the presence of God as never before, and this will change our outlook on life in a very healthy way. Whatever we may be dealing with at a given time, whether it is positive or negative, we will see it in a different light when God is in the picture. Personal relationships thrive on good communication. Increased and improved communication with God in prayer will have a wonderfully beneficial effect on our faith relationship with Him. We will know Him better, feel closer to Him, trust Him more, and long more intensely to be in contact with Him. God is very real to people who pray often.

At the heart of this life-changing communication with God is love—His love for us and our love answering to it. To pray is to reach out for His love, to accept His invitation to know that love, and to live in His love.

Summary

The God who initiates conversation with us is not a stranger. He has known and loved us from all eternity, before we or anything else ever existed. His love is not just a warm feeling for us. It is a firm commitment to do whatever had to be done to save us from the condemnation that we deserve because of our sins and to help us become the kind of people that we were meant to be. This He made indisputably clear by sending Jesus to pay our penalty and win for us the victory. In Jesus, in everything He said, did, and endured, God opened His heart to us and poured out His love. He instills the Holy Spirit in every believer as His love for our continued comfort and support. This love wins our hearts, makes us love Him in return, and moves us to want to communicate with Him.

PRAYER IS THE LANGUAGE OF LOVE.

The essence of prayer is love, God's love embracing us through His Spirit in the implanted Word and our love embracing Him in return. We pray because we know God loves us to the utmost and because we love Him above everyone and everything else. Whatever the content of our prayer conversation with Him, it comes from love and goes to love. All the changes that prayer makes are the product of love. Prayer is the language of love.

Digging Deeper

1. Think about conversations that have changed your life. How has prayer been part of those life-changing conversations?

2. Reflect on your relationships with other people that have developed and grown through a series of conversations. How has your relationship with God changed because of prayer?

3. What would your relationship with God be like if all you heard from Him was demands and accusations?

Learn by Doing

In a private prayer, during a period of silence if you are in a group, pray to God about changes that you would like Him to effect in you or in your life, as well as about those changes that you feel He would like to make. It may be helpful to follow the pattern described in previous chapters by enlarging on the following points:

1. Confess—I am sorry for seeking only changes that interest me and not also those that are important to You, or for not noticing or thanking You for requests You granted.
2. Request—Help me to pray boldly, specifically, and expectantly and to take Your offer seriously to make wonderful changes in and around me. And now I ask You to change this attitude, solve this problem, heal this illness, restore this relationship (be specific).
3. Offer Thanks—Thank You for being there for me, for listening, caring, and acting specifically to answer my request for ________________.
4. Adore—I praise and honor You for Your greatness, Your goodness, and Your willingness to listen.

Notes

____

____

____

____

____

6

Travel Arrangements

A journey's success is often determined by the care and thoroughness with which the arrangements are made, especially for a long, important journey. Occasionally a spontaneous, unplanned trip may turn out well, but most experienced travelers agree that planning and preparation are essential. Unless several key questions are considered, the travel may turn out to be disappointing.

The most important question is why. Why am I taking this journey—to relax, sightsee, have new experiences, transact business, visit someone? If several of these, which has priority? Other questions have to do with the implementation of the answer to this question.

Where? If the purpose is to see someone, the question answers itself. You must go where that person is. However, the other purposes may allow for a variety of options. You may have a choice between desert, mountains, seashore, or among urban, rural, or wilderness settings. In most cases you will also have to reserve overnight accommodations.

When? Weather may be a factor as well as availability of time. The amount of traffic on the highways and at air terminals may determine the time you choose. Health, birthday, or other anniversaries may also affect the time.

How will you get where you want to go? Will you travel by auto, air, train, bicycle, on foot, or by several of the above? These are also important choices. The actions that you take in answer to these questions are the arrangements that will ensure that the journey actually takes place and accomplishes its intended purpose.

If we want our journey into prayer to accomplish its purpose, we will do well to make suitable travel arrangements. It will be helpful to answer and act upon the same questions discussed in the paragraph above.

Digging Deeper

1. Recall an instance in which travel was impaired by lack of adequate arrangements.

   ____

   ____

   ____

   ____

2. Recall a trip that went well because of good advance planning.

   ____

   ____

   ____

   ____

Why Make This Journey into Prayer?

Why do we pray? This was discussed in chapter 2, but we need to return to these questions as we make arrangements for the journey. Why do we want to grow in prayer? What is it that we hope will happen when we pray? Unless we keep our attention centered on the answer to these questions, we may not make appropriate arrangements for the journey, or we may not get very far.

Our purpose in prayer is to approach God to communicate with Him in an open and personal way. We need this, and He welcomes it. Prayer is all about our relationship with God, and that relationship depends significantly on the quality and quantity of our prayer conversation with Him. Thus, it is important to have regular, scheduled prayer times.

IT IS IMPORTANT TO HAVE REGULAR,

SCHEDULED PRAYER TIMES.

In order to flourish, all relationships require some discipline. Unless a husband and wife make time for each other and develop regular ways of helping and pleasing each other, their relationship may stagnate or even decline. Even for couples who have been married for years, it may be healthy to designate Friday nights as "date" nights or to talk on the phone during the noon hour. Similar routines and schedules are helpful for other family relationships and friends. You might frequently have the evening meal with your family or meet with a close friend at least once a month. Spontaneity is also important, but discipline creates the kind of time and contact within which spontaneity can develop.

This is why God commands and expects prayer. It is for the sake of our relationship, and we owe it to Him. He delights in the opportunity to hear from us, and we desperately need the experience of being in His presence and opening up to Him. He is like a parent whose child is going away to college. The parent says, "We want to hear from you a lot. Use your cell phone and e-mail. You can also talk to your friends, but stay in touch with us."

When the phone rings or there is e-mail from the child, the parent receives it eagerly. Even if there is nothing new or urgent in the conversation, it is important to both parent and child. They have touched each other's hearts and lives and grown closer. Our basic motivation in prayer is God's love and promises, but obligation is also present. Our sinful nature is always ready to distract us or cause us to neglect prayer in some other way. God's command to pray reveals that sin and calls us to repentance. Then, His love in Christ draws us back toward Him in prayer.

Digging Deeper

1. How does good communication enhance a relationship?

____

____

____

____

2. How does lack of communication or poor communication erode a relationship?

____

____

____

____

Where Do We Pray?

Most prayers referred to in the Bible were individual and private. As mentioned in the Introduction, that is the way Jesus usually prayed (Mark 1:35; Luke 6:12). He condemned people who made a public spectacle of their prayer (Matthew 6:5; Luke 18:9–14), and He instructed His followers to pray alone behind closed doors (Matthew 6:5–6). This emphasizes the very personal nature of prayer. It encourages openness and intimacy with God and minimizes distraction from other people. In ancient times people usually prayed aloud, which made privacy desirable. But even for us who primarily pray silently, private prayer offers us some of our best opportunities for frank and personal conversation with God.

CORPORATE PRAYER IS ESSENTIAL.

However, corporate prayer is also essential. Christianity is not individualistic. Believers are connected to one another through their common faith in Jesus. We are His Body. He is the Head and we are the members (1 Corinthians 12). Together we worship and work as His extensions in this world. Our function is to help one another grow stronger in faith, obedience, and service. We do this by sharing God's Word with one another in worship, and prayer is an essential part of worship (Ephesians 5:17–20; see also 4:14–16). Members of the first Christian community in Jerusalem "devoted themselves to the apostles' teaching and the fellowship, to the breaking of bread and the prayers. . . . And day by day, attending the temple together and breaking bread [many think that this refers to worship with the Lord's Supper] in their homes, they received their food with glad and generous hearts, praising God and having favor with all the people" (Acts 2:42, 46–47). This snapshot of the life and fellowship of the three thousand new believers who were converted on Pentecost shows that prayer was a major element of their worship together in the temple and in their homes.

Prayer with fellow worshipers is vital to a complete and healthy prayer life. We are encouraged by the presence and participation of others, and we need this. When many pray with believing and attentive hearts for the same things at the same time, God is honored and gives these prayers special attention. Jesus explained that God wants individuals to pray repeatedly for the same thing. This was discussed in chapter 3. Similarly, He also likes it when many people simultaneously lift up their praise and requests. Furthermore, prayers offered in church are carefully prepared and extremely rich in beauty and meaning. Chapter 7 will explore this more.

Digging Deeper

1. How can corporate prayer strengthen private prayer?

When Should We Pray?

As mentioned earlier, communication with God will be more frequent and productive if we have specific times in the day when we regularly pray. If we intend to pray only when we are in the mood for it or when an opportune time arises, we will almost certainly neglect it. We need to look at our lives and decide at what points in the day we will set aside other things, if only very briefly, for personal conversation with God. The Psalms refer to morning and evening prayers (Psalm 5:3; 141:2). By His example, Jesus teaches us to bless food before meals (Luke 9:16; 22:19; 24:30).

These examples suggest a daily schedule that includes at least a brief time of prayer both morning and evening. When morning comes, we thank God for our sleep and for the blessings of the new day. As we think of the opportunities and difficulties that the day will bring, we seek His guidance and strength. At day's end, we reflect on what went wrong, on what we did to offend Him, express our regret, and seek His forgiveness. We ask for restful sleep and protection. Morning and evening prayers do not have to be long, but they should be serious conversations involving a heart and mind open to the implanted Word of God. Prayer at mealtime transforms eating into a time of fellowship with the divine Host.

In addition, we need to schedule perhaps fifteen to thirty minutes each day for personal or family prayer in which prayer is joined with reading and reflection on a portion of Scripture. This is an opportunity to concentrate on the particular issues we face each day with repentance, intercession, thanks, and praise. For maximum benefit this time should be one that is available each day and that is usually free of distraction. Protect that time from other less important activities. Clear your mind and give full attention to your loving God, who is ready and eager to converse with you. The sinful nature will complain that you are just too busy and that you can always work it in later when you have more time. However, all of us know that if the distraction is that important, we would find a way to do it outside of family devotions. We have every reason to make time for regular, scheduled communication with God.

MAKE TIME FOR REGULAR,

SCHEDULED COMMUNICATION WITH GOD.

Digging Deeper

1. About how many minutes of free time do you have on an average day?

2. If you were to follow the suggestions above, how much time would you have for prayer every day?

3. How can we avoid letting scheduled prayer time become forced or unnatural?

How Should We Pray?

How we pray is as important to God as what we pray. He hopes that we will pray from the heart, that we will approach Him in prayer because we love and honor Him. He is not only our almighty God and Lord, He is also a loving and caring friend who is genuinely interested in us and in what we have to say. We approach Him confidently and comfortably because He is our friend, but also reverently and humbly because He is our God. We pray thoughtfully and attentively, relentlessly fighting the temptations to let our minds wander or merely to mouth words mechanically. We pray gratefully, fully aware of the fact that we need this time with God in prayer, even though we do not deserve the privilege of communicating with Him in prayer.

Posture can affect the quality of prayer. No special posture is commanded, but the Bible describes people praying in a variety of positions—standing, kneeling, with or without upraised hands, prostrate on the ground, even in bed during the long night hours when sleep will not come. The practice of closing eyes and folding hands for prayer began in later centuries. Normally, in Bible times people prayed with eyes open but downcast. This variety and openness indicates that the worshiper is free to adopt whatever practice is most meaningful. Kneeling may express humility and reverence; prostration, urgent need; upraised hands, expectation of outpoured blessings; closed eyes, intense concentration; standing, readiness to act obediently; sitting, comfort and security in God's presence. Except in church where worshipers are asked to share a common posture, each person should adopt the most meaningful position for him or her.

Should we use only prayers from a book, or should we always pray spontaneously? There is great value in both kinds of prayer. Prepared prayers are usually more elegant and complete. They remind us to think and pray about things that might otherwise have not occurred to us. They speak to God in ways far more beautiful than we might improvise. However, God does not require prayers that are literary masterpieces. No matter how simple the language or how many grammatical mistakes it has, God welcomes any prayer that comes to Him from a sincere and trusting heart. Prepared prayers can be very helpful in getting us started, but at some point it is important to move beyond someone else's words and thoughts to that which comes from your own heart and life.

GOD WELCOMES ANY PRAYER THAT COMES

TO HIM FROM A SINCERE AND LOVING HEART.

Like a conversation with a loved one or a friend, a prayer conversation with God does not have to be long in order to be valuable. There is certainly a place for lengthy prayers. Jesus prayed all night, and some believers pray for several hours at a time. However, a single sentence plea or exclamation of praise or thanks effectively reaches the heart of God. After a narrow escape from a traffic accident, we might say simply but with great relief, "Thank You, Lord!" Or, after a temper outburst, "Forgive me, Lord, and help me reconcile with the person who angered me." Or, when in danger, "Lord, have mercy!" Jesus makes it clear that our prayers should not be wordy: "And when you pray, do not heap up empty phrases as the Gentiles do, for they think that they will be heard for their many words" (Matthew 6:7). He taught His disciples to pray by giving them the Lord's Prayer, which can be prayed reverently in less than thirty seconds.

We are always to pray in Jesus' name. "Whatever you ask in My name, this I will do, that the Father may be glorified in the Son. If you ask Me anything in My name, I will do it" (John 14:13–14). Therefore, we offer prayer trusting in Him and what He did for us, and we approach the Father on Jesus' merits, not our own. He is the way to the Father, and we cannot reach the Father except through Him (John 14:6). "In Jesus' name" is not just a formality that we include in our prayers; it is the key that opens the line to the Father.

Digging Deeper

1. Under what circumstances is long prayer appropriate?

2. When would a short prayer be appropriate?

Summary

Important as it is, our journey into prayer requires and deserves suitable arrangements. If we thoughtfully consider why, where, when, and how we will make this vital journey, we will be in a position to plan and prepare successfully. To neglect this aspect of the journey is to invite disappointment and regression.

Learn by Doing

Develop a daily schedule of prayer times that is both challenging and realistic. Live by that schedule for a week, evaluate it, and make adjustments.

Notes

Travel Guides

If you are planning a trip to an unfamiliar destination, you may want to take advantage of someone else's knowledge and experience. You may want to talk with someone who has traveled or lived there. You may obtain reading material from a department of tourism, the library, the Internet, or from an individual expert on the area. You may even wish to ask a local person to help you plan your trip and accompany you as your guide. Resources of this kind can transform travel frustration into travel fulfillment.

For our journey into prayer there are some helpful resources that can serve as our travel guides. There are excellent printed materials that have assisted God's people in prayer for many centuries. There are probably some wise and experienced Christian people in your church or your circle of Christian friends who have a heart for prayer and can help others on their journey into prayer. We will consider these resources in this chapter. We will think of them as our tour guides on our journey into prayer. We will do well to take full advantage of them.

The Bible

No better guide to prayer can be found than the Bible itself. And no part of the Bible is more centered in prayer than the Book of Psalms. Most who have a heart for prayer and are strong in prayer extensively use the Psalms. They have been the primary prayer resource for the Church in both public and private worship from the beginning, as they were for God's Old Testament people. Important elements in all Christian liturgies are based on Psalm verses. David and the other psalmists have traveled far on the journey into prayer and can help us make the most of our journey.

Many, but not all, psalms are prayers of various kinds. Others are confessions of faith or statements of truths about God and man. Praise and thanksgiving are the most common themes (Psalm 16, 19, 24, 29, 33, 34, 40, 65, 67, 92, 95, 96, 98, 100, 103, 104, 145, 150). There are also many urgent pleas for help (Psalm 25, 57, 130). Trust and confidence in God are frequently expressed (Psalm 27, 62, 91, 121, 131), and more than a few voice complaints to God (Psalm 73, 77). Although there are frequent references to sin and forgiveness, only a handful are devoted primarily to this (Psalm 6, 32, 38, 51, 130). Several very touching psalms describe the longing of a believer for the presence of God (Psalm 42, 63, 84). Sometimes similar psalms are grouped together, but largely they seem to be arranged randomly.

Although inspired by God, the Psalms also reflect a wide range of human feelings; many reflect personal feelings, and others reflect concerns and issues that all God's people face. Not all sentiments found in the Psalms represent God's will. For example, there are those in which God is called upon to cruelly destroy human enemies. Some of this grows out of respect for God, since the enemies usually defied and mocked Him and His people. However, Jesus has challenged us to love and forgive our enemies, and other psalms remind us that God will deal with those who oppose Him and His people. A large number of Psalms relate to the personal situation of the psalmist or the historical situation of the Jewish people. Thus, we may not identify with everything in every psalm, but we must fit them to our situation when we pray them, or, in some cases, use such verses for purposes other than prayer.

In view of this complexity, the Psalms may seem difficult to use in personal prayer. However, the person who patiently prays through them, a few each day, will discover them to be a priceless resource. Some psalms will immediately become favorites. Others will eventually grow on the one who prays them. Today my mood and needs will be met by certain psalms, and tomorrow I will tune into others. The person who prays an average of six psalms each day will pray them all in one month and soon will know where to turn for those that fit the present moment. In my experience, the more I pray the Psalms, the more I want to pray them.

Who could be a better guide for devotional use of the Psalms than Martin Luther, who not only studied, taught and wrote about them, but also used them faithfully and gratefully all his life? *Reading the Psalms with Luther* (St. Louis: Concordia, 2007) offers a brief commentary by Luther on each psalm, relating its themes both to the current situation as well as to the Catechism. This is followed by a brief prayer. It is in an inviting and user-friendly format.

There are some powerful examples elsewhere in the Bible of believing prayer. Abraham prayed for the son God had promised (Genesis 15:2–3). David expressed his overwhelming gratitude for the blessings God had bestowed on him, the nation, and his family (2 Samuel 7:18–29). Hezekiah earnestly begged God to deliver His people from the Assyrian armies (2 Kings 19:14–19). Jonah thanked God profusely after being rescued from the belly of the big fish (Jonah 2:2–9).

Then, in the New Testament, we have Jesus' own prayers on the night before He died, which He offered for the Church (John 17) and for deliverance from the ordeal of the cross (Matthew 26:36–42). After Peter was miraculously released from prison, the believers prayed gratefully and confidently (Acts 4:23–31). Paul prayed continuously and thankfully for the Ephesian Christians and for the help they would need in order to remain faithful (Ephesians 1:15–23). John describes how the inhabitants of heaven are joined by every creature in the universe in the praise of God's Son for His work of redemption (Revelation 5:6–14). Prayers like these can inspire and motivate us for our own journey into prayer.

Digging Deeper

1. Read and meditate on each of the following psalms. In what ways do they speak from your heart and life? What adjustments are needed to fit your situation?

   Psalm 103 (Praise and Thanksgiving)

   Psalm 130 (Help)

   Psalm 121 (Trust and Confidence)

   Psalm 51 (Sin and Forgiveness)

   ____

   ____

   ____

   ____

2. Read the prayer of the believers after they were threatened for preaching about Jesus and then released (Acts 4:23–31). What is striking about the content of their prayer? What would you have prayed in their situation?

   ____

   ____

   ____

   ____

   ____

Hymns

An often overlooked resource for prayer is the hymns of the Church. In most hymnals, 20 percent or more of the hymns are poetic prayers set to music. The words of these hymns come from the hearts and experiences of gifted and sensitive believers who have learned to express their needs and thanks to God with language that is reverently beautiful. Often, hymns are rich with meaning and allusions to Scripture. When we sing them in church, we may have difficulty grasping everything that is in them, especially if the music moves briskly. However, if we use them in private and family devotion, either spoken or sung, and give thoughtful attention to what they are saying, we can pray them with meaning. If we make it a point to arrive for church worship a few minutes early, we will have an opportunity to meditate on the prayer hymns and prepare to sing them more beneficially. Along with Bibles there should be one or more hymnals in every Christian home as travel guides for the journey into prayer.

There are prayer hymns for virtually every season, situation, or need. Christmas, Easter, and Pentecost have inspired many. There are confession and forgiveness hymns; praise and thanksgiving hymns; trust, commitment, and hope hymns. There are hymns for morning and for evening, for times of suffering and for times of joy. The variety is great. Those who want to grow in prayer will do well to spend time with a hymnal, exploring its contents for the kinds of prayer hymns that will enrich their communication with God. One example of a splendid prayer hymn is the following:

Son of God, eternal Savior,
Source of life and truth and grace,
Word made flesh, whose birth among us
Hallows all our human race,
You our Head, who, throned in glory,

For Your own will ever plead:
Fill us with Your love and pity,
Heal our wrongs, and help our need.

As You, Lord, have lived for others,
So may we for others live.
Freely have Your gifts been granted;
Freely may Your servants give.
Yours the gold and Yours the silver,
Yours the wealth of land and sea;
We but stewards of Your bounty
Held in solemn trust will be.

Come, O Christ, and reign among us,
King of love and Prince of Peace;
Hush the storm of strife and passion,
Bid its cruel discords cease.
By Your patient years of toiling,
By Your silent hours of pain,
Quench our fevered thirst of pleasure,
Stem our selfish greed of gain.

Son of God, eternal Savior,
Source of life and truth and grace,
Word made flesh, whose birth among us
Hallows all our human race:
By Your praying, by Your willing
That Your people should be one,
Grant, O grant our hope's fruition:
Here on earth Your will be done. (LSB 842)

Digging Deeper

1. What are some sins for which we seek help in this hymn?

2. What change in heart and life is emphasized in this hymn?

3. What enables Jesus to implement this change?

Other Resources

In addition to prayers in the Bible and hymnals there are also some other good published materials. Christian bookstores usually have hundreds of books devoted to prayer as well as a wide variety of devotional books that include prayers. In addition, a few books consist almost entirely of prayers for different occasions and needs, sometimes written by a single author, while others collect prayers from numerous authors across the centuries. Unless it is a store identified with your church body, the materials may not always conform to your understanding and beliefs. Evaluating the material with your pastor or some other knowledgeable person is helpful.

A valuable guide and support for your journey into prayer is a good prayer book, one with which you can identify and which you will enjoy using. As mentioned in the last chapter, a growing and meaningful prayer life is best served by a combination of prepared and self-composed prayer. As we thoughtfully use prayers from a book, we will be moved to pray about things that we would never have thought to include and may find satisfaction in addressing God with language richer and more beautiful than anything that we might be able to say. For more than forty years I have used a marvelous prayer book designed especially for pastors, and I have come to treasure and welcome it along with my own spontaneous prayers.

Recently, I became attached to a small work with the interesting title: *The Complete Idiot's Guide to Christian Prayers and Devotions*, by James S. Bell Jr. and Tracy Macon Sumner (Indianapolis, IN: Alpha, 2008). It is a useful collection of prayers from many sources along with brief devotions and explanatory comments.

Portals of Prayer, published quarterly by Concordia Publishing House, contains an excellent assortment of prayers along with Bible references and brief daily messages.

A new major and well-received resource is *Treasury of Daily Prayer* (St. Louis: Concordia, 2008). The Introduction explains that it "is designed to meet the needs of the Christian who wishes to follow a disciplined order of daily prayer centered in the Scriptures. It employs the rich resources of liturgy, hymnody, prayer, writings from the Church Fathers and the Confessions." Scripture passages, prayers, and writings for each day, as well as additional prayers and devotional helps are printed out for the convenience of the worshiper. This makes for a book of many pages, which requires a bit of figuring out. At first this may seem daunting, but by the second day it proves to be very user-friendly. The basic program for each day can be completed in 15 minutes, leaving time, even for a busy person, to reflect and meditate or to use the supplementary materials that are provided.

An additional resource that I have come to appreciate greatly and heartily recommend is *The Book of a Thousand Prayers*, compiled by Angela Ashwin (Grand Rapids, MI: Zondervan, 2002). This anthology of prayers by hundreds of different authors throughout Christian history is arranged in categories that enable readers to find something to address what is on their heart in various situations and for various needs. Most are prayers related to personal life, but others also speak to issues in the church, the community, and the world. Explicitly or implicitly, they reflect a commitment to the Gospel and the Bible. Like a number of the Psalms, it may take you a while to get used to some of these prayers, and you may never feel comfortable with others. However, the vast majority are helpful and worth incorporating into your prayer journey. One example on page 33 is by Augustine of Hippo, one of the greatest of all Christian thinkers and writers:

> *Almighty God, you have made us for yourself, and our hearts are restless until they find rest in you. Grant us purity of heart and strength of purpose, that no selfish passion may hinder us from knowing your will, and no weakness hinder us from doing it; but that in your light we may see light, and in your service find our perfect freedom; through Jesus Christ our Lord.*

Digging Deeper

1. What language or thought in the above prayer can you readily understand and make your own? Why?

____

____

____

2. What language or thought is unclear or outside your experience? Why?

Learn by Doing

Carefully read through any six of the psalms listed on page 68. From them, select two for use in your prayers for the next week. After praying through each psalm, add something about your own thoughts and concerns.

Notes

8

Travel Companions

The benefit and enjoyment of a journey can be magnified if it is shared with the right companion. One will notice and delight in what the other overlooked. Problems and disappointments can be tolerable when faced together. Not only during the journey but also afterward travel companions can relive their experiences with as much pleasure as when it all took place.

The same can be said of our journey into prayer. Companions can add a lot to our prayer experience. Chapter 6 pointed out that it is as important to pray with others is as it is to pray alone. Prayer with others in church was also discussed. There, all of our fellow worshipers are our companions in prayer. Whenever we use a prayer prepared by someone else, whether a psalm, a hymn, or something from a book of prayers, the author is our companion in prayer. The prayers we send to God are joined with those of the redeemed already with Him, as well as with those of the angels, so that all the hosts of heaven are also our prayer companions. As we make our journey into prayer, we are surrounded by a great throng of people who are also on this pilgrimage.

In this chapter we are considering some other travel companions whom we can join. There are three types, each with its own special value: prayer partners, prayer groups, and prayer chains. None of these are divinely required, and they may not be for you. However, in the experience of many Christians, they are helpful and worth your consideration.

Digging Deeper

1. What are some situations in which you would prefer to travel alone?

2. What are some situations in which you would prefer to pray alone?

Prayer Partners

Often, a program of growth or improvement will be more successful if it is done with a partner. If you decided to walk for exercise with a friend, your chances of remaining consistent are considerably better than if you did it by yourself. You would remind, encourage, and feel a certain commitment to each other. A prayer partner can provide similar support for your journey into prayer.

The term "prayer partner" is used in several different ways. Christian mission and service agencies designate interested people who support their work with prayer and money as prayer partners. Web sites offer prayer partner agreements that connect people with individuals who will pray with them or for them. Depending on whom you are dealing with, these may be valid and valuable uses of prayer. Other similar examples of prayer partners exist.

What is suggested here is more personal and related to the fellowship of your congregation. As you continue your journey into prayer, identify someone who seems to have a special interest and a heart for prayer. Explore with that person the possibility of meeting together regularly for prayer. This might be someone you already know and to whom you are close—a friend, relative, or spouse. However, it could also be someone less familiar, to whom you could grow closer over time. The level of intimacy could rise as you learn to know and trust each other. Partnership of this kind involves the sharing of personal information. Consequently, this should be a person with the maturity and integrity to honor the confidential nature of this relationship. In addition, this relationship should be God-pleasing without violating another relationship such as marriage.

In your prayer time together you would pray for each other and for those whose needs and concerns have come to your attention—family, friends, church, and world. Specifically notice the blessings God has poured out on you, others, the church, and the world and praise and thank Him for them. Seek pardon for what is going wrong in your own hearts and lives. Listen to what God has said by beginning your time together with appropriate Scripture, especially the Psalms, and by reminding each other what God has said through what you have previously read and heard. Friendly conversation would be an important element, but for you to be partners in prayer, the emphasis has to be on prayer.

It could take some effort and time to enlist a prayer partner, but such a person is a valuable companion on your journey into prayer. You might also have to get over your inhibition to pray aloud with another person, but that is well worth it too. Until we get through that barrier, we deprive ourselves of the growth in prayer attainable in this kind of relationship.

Digging Deeper

1. What anxieties or misgivings might discourage you from seeking a prayer partner?

2. What potential benefits might encourage you?

Prayer Groups

A prayer group is essentially an expanded prayer partnership. For a prayer partnership to grow into a prayer group involving three to six people is a very healthy development. Although there may be less intimacy, there may also be more support and greater diversity of gifts and insights. From their lives and experience, the members will come to the group with his or her own sorrows, joys, weaknesses, strengths, concerns, hopes, doubts, successes, and failures. As one member brings these to God and to the group in prayer, the other members add their supporting petitions, and from God's Word implanted in their hearts and minds, they offer their perception of what He has to say in response to these requests. In this way, each member's prayers are augmented and enriched by the prayers and witness of the other members, and the strength of the requests is magnified.

The existence of a prayer group in a congregation makes a statement about the importance and value of prayer. It can be a comfort to other members to know that, if they need prayer for any special reason, there are people in their church ready and willing to offer it in their behalf. Others can be encouraged to submit prayer requests in writing, by telephone, e-mail, or in person before the group.

As with a prayer partnership, a prayer group may develop slowly, especially if this is the first time one has been established. Members of the congregation need to get acquainted with the idea before they can become interested in joining or submitting prayer requests to the group. Those who feel led to found the group or help it to grow may find both individual and general invitations effective. No matter how small the group or how few the prayer requests, a group that continues meeting, praying, and inviting might well become a vital aspect of congregational life.

Digging Deeper

1. Have you ever asked anyone to pray for you? Have others asked you to pray for them? Under what circumstances?

2. Who do you think would be good in a prayer group? How would you feel about being part of that group?

Prayer Chains

When a group of mountain climbers ascends steep, rugged mountains or sheer rock cliffs, they usually link together with a cable so that if one slips or falls, the cable enables them to recover. A prayer chain meets the need for prayer in a similar way. A prayer chain is a group of believers linked together by a commitment to pray on request for all who need it. There may be one or more such chains in a congregation.

Each chain consists of twelve members or fewer. A list of names, phone numbers, and perhaps e-mail addresses is drawn up. When prayer is requested, the person at the head of the list is notified. He or she prays for the one mentioned in the request and then contacts the next person who does the same, and so on until everyone in the chain has honored the request. In this way, anyone who needs and wants prayer can be assured that a group of fellow believers with a heart for prayer has brought the need to the throne of God.

In this electronic age when e-mail often receives better attention than phone messages, a prayer vine might be even more effective. In this arrangement, one person receives prayer requests and immediately sends them by e-mail to everyone on the prayer vine list. This eliminates the interruptions sometimes experienced with a prayer chain. This is an effective but simple way to initiate serious prayer when prayer is needed.

Digging Deeper

1. What are some problems that could hinder a prayer chain?

2. How might these problems be solved?

Summary

On some parts of our journey into prayer we travel alone, as Jesus did when He withdrew from the crowds and from His disciples in order to be alone with the heavenly Father. All of us need quality one-on-one time with God. There are things that we need to say to Him and hear from Him that are for no one else's ears.

Yet, there are times in which travel companions are important, as they were to Jesus, who prayed both with and for His followers. Some of us are private while others are more social, and this will affect the way we respond to opportunities for travel companions on our prayer journey. However, even those who are more private can be blessed and be a blessing if they make some use of travel companions on their journey into prayer.

Learn by Doing

Ask someone, perhaps a close Christian friend or family member, to pray for you aloud in your presence. Offer to do the same.

Notes

9

Journey without End

If a journey surpasses your expectations, if the transportation, accommodations, places, and people make it happy, comfortable, and interesting, you might wish the journey would never end. However, as the old saying goes: "All good things must come to an end." We accept that as an absolute because life is just that way so often.

Our journey into prayer is an exception. This journey can keep right on going and get even better as we go along. The journey into prayer travels into the presence of God for the purpose of serious and personal conversation. As we grow in our prayer life and enter God's presence more frequently, the quality of the conversation can improve noticeably. In this life our journey into prayer will never be perfect because of our sinfulness, but it can improve. And, when this life is over, the journey will not deteriorate or end, but will continue at a level of joy, comfort, security, interest, and fulfillment that will make any other journey seem pathetic by comparison.

"Pray without ceasing . . ." (1 Thessalonians 5:17).

This passage and others like it tell us that our journey into prayer should never be interrupted (see also Luke 18:1; Romans 1:9–10; Ephesians 6:18; Colossians 1:3; 1 Thessalonians 1:3; 2:13; 2 Timothy 1:3). How are we to understand this? How are we to put this into practice? Some Christians have thought this means they should withdraw from ordinary life and spend all of their time at prayer. This cannot be what St. Paul means. He himself was fully involved in ordinary life as a tentmaker, traveling missionary, and author. Elsewhere, he tells believers to work for a living, tend their families, encourage one another, and bear witness to the world. All these things require time, effort, and concentration. How can we be praying continually if we are doing these things?

St. Paul himself gives us the answer: "So, whether you eat or drink, or whatever you do, do all to the glory of God" (1 Corinthians 10:31). In another place he adds to this: "And whatever you do, in word or deed, do everything in the name of the Lord Jesus, giving thanks to God the Father through Him" (Colossians 3:17). He gives a striking application of this in Ephesians 6:5–8. There, he tells slaves that they should serve their masters with respect, fear, and sincerity of heart, just as if they were serving Christ. They should regard even menial and unpleasant work as an opportunity to do something for their Lord.

What he is describing is a life lived for God in every aspect. Whatever we must or choose to do, we are urged to do it in a way that pleases and honors Him. Daily life can be a prayer of thanks and praise to God, even those parts of life that seem mundane or tedious. You can take a shower to the glory of God, not only to make yourself more comfortable but also to show appreciation to your Creator by taking care of your body and by being considerate of other people whom you will be around. You can eat your breakfast to the glory of God, not only as a source of energy for the day but also as an opportunity to acknowledge the One who has provided the food and made it so pleasing to eat. Whether at work or at home, you can recognize God's part and will in each task, and you can do it as to Him. You can read a book, watch television, go fishing or hunting, or play golf as an act of worship to God. They will be worship if they are activities of which He approves and if you do them to please Him.

DAILY LIFE CAN BE A PRAYER OF THANKS AND PRAISE TO GOD.

Daily life can have this prayerful quality and significance if we are aware of God, His presence, His interest, and His involvement in whatever we think or do. This is what living in the presence of God means. It involves intentionally drawing God into the ongoing current of thoughts and feelings flowing through our consciousness. As we do this, God can powerfully influence our ideas, emotions, and desires, and He enables us to see Him in the faces of the people with whom we interact and to respond to them in His own wonderful way.

Our consciousness of God and our grateful submission to God will transform daily life into a continuous and powerful statement of praise to God. It will bring honor and pleasure to God as others become more aware of Him through the difference that He makes in us. We are praying continually when this is how we live. A poet has put it vividly. He prays to the Holy Spirit:

Breathe on Thy cloven Church once more,

That in these gray and latter days

There may be those whose life is praise,

Each life a high doxology

To Father, Son, and unto Thee.

(Martin H. Franzmann, LSB 834:4)

In the course of every day, there are also many other marvelous opportunities for prayer, and we should be quick to take advantage of them. While walking, driving, or waiting for an appointment, we all have free time at our disposal. Instead of giving in to boredom or irritation, or instead of passing the time with a magazine or television, we can seize these minutes as opportunities for prayer. We can fill them with lively conversation with God. Pray for the people around you. Notice and give thanks for the blessings in the situation. Ask God what He thinks and how He feels about what is going on in and around you. Express regret for your sins of irritation or impatience that you are experiencing and receive His pardon. Praise Him for His availability and readiness to fill not only these minutes but also your entire life with His presence. Used in this way, free minutes become some of the most precious moments of the day.

SEIZE . . . OPPORTUNITIES FOR PRAYER.

For many of us, even the night hours include empty times that invite prayer. When sleep will not come, instead of tossing and turning, we can discover in such wakefulness God's invitation to pray. Insomnia can be a very lonely experience. Others in the family and in the community are sound asleep, and you seem to be the only one awake. Your mind may be racing, and you may be tense with frustration and distress, dreading the day ahead that you will have to face without adequate sleep. Or, you might sleep for an hour or two, awaken, and have trouble falling asleep again.

These periods of sleeplessness are valuable opportunities for close, personal communication with God. God is right there, eager to break through into your thoughts, to share your anxieties and frustration, to assure you of His presence and His love, and to give you His peace. In effect, what He is saying to us at such a time is, "I will keep you company. I will get you through this night and tomorrow. I can and will deal with anything that is worrying you." Long hours of wakefulness are not wasted if they are spent in this kind of prayer. They become a rewarding, refreshing, and strengthening experience. In Psalm 63:6–8, David describes his insomniac communication with God: "I remember You upon my bed, and meditate on You in the watches of the night; for You have been my help, and in the shadow of Your wings I will sing for joy. My soul clings to You; Your right hand upholds me."

God also gives us the opportunity to get rid of the things that are keeping us awake, to cast all our "anxieties on Him, because He cares for you" (1 Peter 5:7). Accept this offer, saying, "Lord, there is nothing I can do about any of these things that are disturbing my rest. But You can, so I am putting all of them into Your hands. Please do not let Satan bring them back." With that, in my experience, sleep is usually quick to come.

PRAY CONTINUALLY!

"Pray continually!" is neither unrealistic nor burdensome. It can be done with actions as well as with thoughts and words. Not only does it express and foster a closer relationship with God, but it also makes life far more interesting and hopeful than would otherwise be possible.

Digging Deeper

1. What makes it difficult to live your daily life as a prayer to God?

____

____

____

2. What free times in your life will prayer most easily fill?

____

____

____

A Journey into Eternity

In the life to come, because of what Jesus did and endured for us, we will experience the presence of God as never before and be able to converse with Him more openly, intimately, and delightfully than ever before. And this relationship and the prayer communication that is so important to it will never end.

It is impossible for us to fully imagine the difference that will take place in our relationship to God once we join Him in heaven. For the first time our relationship will be untroubled by sin and doubt. All those roadblocks and everything like it will be left behind. We will enjoy closeness and comfort in His presence that we have never known here. We will see God face-to-face in all of His glory and majesty. We will experience the fullness of His love for us. From this perfect bond with our God will come peace, happiness, and security beyond description.

In that relationship, communication will be enhanced immeasurably. Some of the content will be wonderfully different. With sin no longer in our hearts and lives we will never again have to tell God that we are sorry, and He will never have to tell us that we are forgiven. With danger and trouble no longer in the picture we will never again have to cry out to Him for help, and He will never have to comfort or assure us of His help. Concerns of this kind that are so much a part of our prayers now will no longer enter our conversations with Him.

Does that mean we will have nothing to talk about? Not at all. Our words and thoughts to God will be full of love, thanks, and praise for all that He is, does, and means to us. In Revelation, the apostle John is given a vision of heaven and of the worship that is offered to God (Revelation 4; 5; 7). It is all thanksgiving and praise, extravagant and uninhibited, that delights God, exhilarates His people, and explodes from hearts bursting with love for Him. Do not think of this as something formal and ceremonial, but rather as spontaneous, creative, and passionate celebrations of God's greatness, glory, and love. It also celebrates our status as His children who are overwhelmed by His endless generosity.

Summary

In addition to this thrilling collective communication with all the hosts of heaven, we will have unlimited access for personal, one-on-one conversation with God. God is not only interested in us as members of that huge family, but He also knows and loves us as individuals and wants to relate to us personally. Although there is only one of Him, He is able and eager to relate and converse with all of us individually, and you will be thrilled to take advantage of this. We all have an abundance of personal reasons to offer God our praise and thanks. We all have many unanswered questions that we want to ask Him. We will all want to express our love to Him personally. We will be able to do this freely, openly, and confidently. Everything that now limits and hinders our relationship with God and makes conversation halting and uncomfortable will no longer get in the way. By His sacrifice Christ removed not only the guilt of our sin but also its power to interfere with prayer. Already in this life He begins to counteract Satan's efforts to clog the lines between us and our Father. In the next life, the lines will always be completely clear and the communication perfect.

Digging Deeper

1. What change in your relationship with God in the life to come will encourage communication the most?

   ____

   ____

   ____

2. What are some questions you would like God to answer?

Learn by Doing

Imagine yourself stuck in traffic. In that situation, what could you bring to God in prayer?

Notes

10

Conclusion

We have covered the basics of prayer:

- Problems and obstacles that interfere with prayer
- The purpose of prayer
- Our side of the conversation
- God's side of the conversation
- How God responds to our prayer
- Arranging our lives to accommodate prayer
- Resources for prayer
- Praying with others
- Praying continually now and in the life to come

We have studied what God's Word says about these basics. We have reflected on them, discussed them, and developed some new attitudes, expectations, and skills. All this can help us make progress on our journey into prayer.

To make the most of our journey into prayer—to keep strong, growing, and engaged—we have to keep returning to the basics. No matter how much progress we make, there will also be times when we stall, when interest and involvement sag, and when we seem to be right back where we started. Especially at such times it is important to return to the basics.

When his team is in a slump, a wise coach will have his players give special attention to pitching, batting, fielding, and base running—the basics. When performance becomes erratic or lifeless, the wise musician will practice scales—the basics. When his audiences become restless and inattentive, the wise speaker will review content, organization of material, illustrations, and delivery—the basics. When a marital relationship goes stale, wise spouses will devote more time and attention to each other—the basics.

However, even when the journey seems to be going well, it is important periodically to return to the basics. We need to ask ourselves: What in my life could interfere with prayer, and how can I prevent that from happening? Why am I praying? What is the purpose? To whom am I talking? What is He like? What is His attitude toward me? How does He respond? How can I make time and opportunity for prayer? Who and what can help me pray? This kind of analysis and evaluation helps to keep our prayer journey on track.

We have compelling reasons for getting more serious and active in prayer. Our loving God made us for a close and personal relationship with Him, and prayer fosters this. By sacrificing Himself, God's Son, Jesus, gained access for us into the Father's presence. The Holy Spirit within us is constantly urging us to pray and is always ready to help us (Romans 8:26–27). Thus, we can grow in our prayer life. We can travel further on this journey. And we should. The God who makes this possible also commands us to do this and promises to receive and respond to our prayers.

So pray. Begin to pray more often and more attentively. Pray boldly, specifically, and expectantly. Start somewhere, anywhere, and proceed step-by-step toward a richer prayer life. Regard this as a learning experience that will include setbacks as well as successes. Be prepared to struggle against the devil and everything he will do to interfere.

Your first step may be to identify a small block of time somewhere during your day in which you can devote undivided and undisturbed attention to God's Word and prayer. Or, it may be securing a hymnal or book of prayers, watching for empty minutes that each day brings and using them for prayer, or turning your self-talk into lively conversation with God. From that beginning, keep adding additional dimensions until you can notice and celebrate the difference in your prayer life.

Whatever it takes, it is worth it. A life lived in the presence of God and in ongoing conversation with Him is happier, more interesting, secure, confident, and hopeful than one in which God rarely breaks into our awareness. Even when we endure hard and frightening experiences, we can meet them convinced that He is there with compassion, support, and guidance, and we know we can talk to Him about them and that He will listen and respond. This realization turns adversity into blessing. Furthermore, the joys and successes that come our way are magnified infinitely when we recognize them as God's gifts of love.

In some respects, the journey into prayer is long, but it is also immensely rewarding and one of the most important journeys you will ever take. A Chinese proverb says that the longest journey begins with a single step. That step into prayer and all that follow can make a marvelous difference in your life.